P9-DID-667

JUDO

NEIL MORRIS

HEINEMANN LIBRARY
CHICAGO, ILLINOIS

© 2001 Reed Educational & Professional Publishing
Published by Heinemann Library,
an imprint of Reed Educational & Professional Publishing,
Chicago, Illinois

Customer Service 888-454-2279

Visit our website at www.heinemannlibrary.com

Designed by Ken Vail Graphic Design, Cambridge
Illustrations by Simon Girling & Associates (Mike Lacey)
Originated by Dot Gradations
Printed by Wing King Tong in Hong Kong

05 04 03 02 01
10 9 8 7 6 5 4 3 2 1

Library of Congress Cataloging-in-Publication Data
Morris, Neil, 1946-
    Judo.
        p. cm. -- (Get going! Martial arts)
    Includes bibliographical references and index.
    ISBN 1-58810-038-3
    1. Judo--Juvenile literature. [1. Judo.]   I. Title.
GV1114 .M67 2001
796.815'2--dc21

00-013092

J 796.8152
MORR

Acknowledgments
The Publishers would like to thank the following for permission to reproduce photographs:
Action Images/Tim Matthews, p. 8.; Bob Willingham, pp. 5, 6, 7, 21, 27, 28. All other photographs by Trevor Clifford.

Cover photograph reproduced with permission of Empics.

Every effort has been made to contact copyright holders of any material reproduced in this book. Any omissions will be rectified in subsequent printings if notice is given to the Publisher.

The Publisher would like to thank Dr. Kei Narimatsu for helping us improve the accuracy of this text.

Some words are shown in bold, **like this.** You can find out what they mean by looking in the glossary.

32530 60547 1927

Japanese words are shown in italics, *like this.* You can find out what they mean by looking at the chart on page 30.

CONTENTS

! Please remember that martial arts need to be taught by a qualified, registered teacher. Do not try the techniques or movements in this book without an instructor present.

WHAT IS JUDO?

Judo is a Japanese martial art in which students, called *judokas*, use throwing and **grappling** techniques. The word *judo* means "gentle way." This is a good description of the art, because much of its skill lies in using balanced techniques to overcome an opponent. Like other martial arts, judo offers the chance to practice demanding physical routines, to take part in a competitive sport, and to learn about self-defense.

People who know little about judo may think of it as a rough, or even violent sport. But in judo, no one ever tries to hurt an opponent. It is the "gentle way" because many techniques depend on the *judoka* apparently giving in to an opponent's attack until it is the right moment to strike back.

The founder of judo, Jigoro Kano, believed that judo allowed a smaller, lighter, weaker person to overcome a larger, heavier, stronger opponent. For example, if the more powerful *judoka* tries to push his or her opponent, the less powerful *judoka* can move back quickly and not lose his or her balance. Then the person who is pushing forward is off balance and can easily be thrown down.

Young judokas test each other's strength and balance.

MENTAL DISCIPLINE

Judo is a form of exercise that uses the mind as well as the body. Its founder believed that *judokas* could train themselves to achieve "maximum efficiency with minimum effort" by coordinating mind and body in attack and defense. The example on page 4 is a good illustration of this balance. A *judoka* must always be alert, controlled, and calm, ready to react to any situation. Both competitors should get something out of judo, rather than simply being a winner or a loser.

WHERE TO LEARN AND PRACTICE

This book gives you lots of ideas about how to get started in judo. It also shows and explains some judo techniques, so that you can understand and practice them. But always remember that you cannot learn a martial art just from a book. To study judo seriously, you must go to regular lessons with a qualified teacher. You must learn all the techniques properly, and then repeat and practice them many times.

YOUR JUDO CLUB

Choose your club carefully. It should have an experienced teacher and belong to a judo association. The addresses on page 31 are sources for gathering information about clubs.

These students are in a modern judo club.

JUDO—THE BEGINNINGS

Judo developed from an ancient Japanese form of unarmed combat, physical training, and self-defense called *jujitsu*, which means "gentle skill." *Jujitsu*, or hand-to-hand combat, was practiced centuries ago by *samurai* who learned the skills involved in *jujitsu* along with archery, swordsmanship, and spear fighting. Monks, merchants, and travelers were also trained in *jujitsu*. Original *jujitsu* included techniques such as kicking and choking, which could be used to fight off and disable an opponent.

In 1882, a young Japanese man named Jigoro Kano turned *jujitsu* into a modern martial art, which he called judo. When Kano was eleven, his family moved from the country to Tokyo, which had just been made the **imperial** capital of Japan. Kano was small for his age, and at first he was bullied at his new school. He decided to learn *jujitsu* as a means of self-defense. After doing so, his new-found confidence and physical skills kept him from ever being picked on again.

Jigoro Kano (1860–1938) was the founder of judo.

After continuing to train in *jujitsu* while studying at Tokyo University, Kano decided to take its best features and turn them into a means of personal development. He removed the dangerous kicks and punches, introduced regular practice in falling techniques, and drew up a set of rules for all judo students. He named his new school *Kodokan,* meaning "the place for studying the way." When Tokyo's chief of police organized a contest between *Kodokan* judo students and traditional *jujitsu* schools, Kano's pupils won.

The Kodokan International Judo Center in Tokyo has more than a million visitors each year. Inside is a Judo Hall of Fame.

By 1887, the *Kodokan* school had more than 1,500 pupils. Judo's popularity quickly grew throughout Japan, where it soon was taught in schools. In 1889, Jigoro Kano traveled to Europe to spread his **philosophy.** The popularity of judo quickly spread worldwide, especially in Europe. Interest in judo was increased in the United States because of the enthusiasm that President Theodore Roosevelt showed for the martial art. Kano also believed that judo was good for women. He opened special training halls for them, despite severe criticism at the time.

After Jigoro Kano's death, interest in his martial art continued to grow quickly and judo became a major competitive sport. It became an Olympic sport in 1964.

EQUIPMENT

Judo is performed in a special outfit called a *judogi,* or *gi* (sounds like *gee*). It is best to buy a *gi* through your judo club. The *judogi* is usually all white, but in some high-level competitions, one of the two competitors wears a blue *judogi.*

The *judogi* is made up of a pair of trousers and a loose jacket tied at the waist with a belt. Girls wear a white T-shirt under the jacket. *Gis* are usually sold with a white belt, which is the right color for a beginner. The *gi* has stronger material across the shoulders, around the collar, and at the knees so that it is not easily torn.

The blue judogi *is worn only for high-level competitions.*

Always keep your *gi* clean and neat, and wash it after each training session. A neat and tidy appearance shows that you have the right attitude toward training. Inside the training hall, called a *dojo,* you must always have bare feet. Shoes would damage the *tatami* mat on which all judo exercises are practiced.

PUTTING ON THE GI

1 Put the trousers on first. Pull the drawstring and tie it in a bow. Next, put on the jacket, crossing the left side over the right side.

2 To tie the belt, pull it across your stomach, keeping the two ends of an equal length.

3 Cross the ends behind your back and bring them back to the front.

4 Cross the left end over the right, then pull it up behind both layers of the belt.

5 Tie the free ends together, right over left, and pull them through to finish the knot.

⚠ SAFETY

In order not to harm yourself or anyone else, do not wear a watch or any jewelry. Keep your fingernails and toenails trimmed short. Pull long hair back, but do not use metal clips.

Make sure that you are in good shape for active exercise, and do not train if you are ill. Exercise should not hurt, so never push yourself to a point at which you feel pain.

Any martial art can be dangerous if it is not performed properly. Never fool around inside or outside the training hall—or at home or in school—by showing off or pretending to have a real fight.

IN THE DOJO

TRADITIONAL COURTESY

It is important for any *judoka* to show respect to everyone and everything related to judo. Polite behavior and discipline are of great importance in all martial arts. Judo students must show respect and courtesy to opponents, other students, and to the art of judo itself. Everyone must learn the rules and courtesies of judo. In the *dojo,* the word of the *sensei,* the judo instructor, is law.

To begin a session, students make a kneeling bow to their *sensei.* To do this, first kneel down on the floor. Point your toes and sit back on your calves, keeping your back straight and looking forward. Then bend forward, sliding your hands down your thighs and onto the mat just in front of your knees. Let your eyes follow the bow to the floor, but do not let your face get too close to the mat.

The kneeling bow shows great respect.

Before and after every practice, and each time they change partners within a practice session, *judokas* make a standing bow to one another. All *judokas,* from beginners to Olympic finalists, make this bow to begin and end each contest.

To make the bow, stand in a relaxed way, looking straight ahead. Your feet should be about a shoulder-width apart, with your hands relaxed at your sides. You then bow smoothly by bending your upper body forward slightly. Let your eyes follow the bow to the floor, and slide your hands forward so that the palms cover your knees. Hold the position for a second, then straighten up again.

When you are bowing to a partner, make sure there is enough space between you so that you do not bump heads. One and a half arms' distance is usually about right.

This is a standing bow made by two partners.

KATA CONTESTS

Kata, meaning "form," is a demonstration of prearranged judo techniques, performed by a *judoka* with a cooperating partner. The techniques are linked together by a common theme. Each of the themes is based on one of 21 techniques originally used by ancient warriors. There are *kata* contests and championships, and *kata* is also used at grading exams for promotions.

WARMING UP

Judo involves a lot of hard, physical exercise. As with all exercise, it is important to warm up your body and stretch your muscles before training. At your club, you will always start a session with at least ten to fifteen minutes of warm-up exercises. You might begin by walking or jogging in place for a couple of minutes before doing some stretching exercises.

! IMPORTANT

- Drink a lot of water, and do not exercise too hard when it is very hot or humid.

- Do not exercise when you are ill or injured.

- Try not to breathe too hard and fast when you are exercising or resting.

- Do not hold your breath while you are exercising.

- When you are stretching, you should always remain comfortable, and your muscles should not hurt. If you feel pain, stop at once.

- You should begin to exercise immediately after warming up. You should do some cool-down exercises immediately after exercising.

WINDMILLS

Turn your arms like the sails of a windmill.

1 Stand up straight with your arms by your sides.

2 Swing your right arm forward, up, and around behind you in a circle. Keep your arm straight and reach high at the top of the circle. Repeat five times.

3 Do the same exercise with the left arm.

4 Then repeat the exercise, working both arms at the same time.

CALF STRETCH

The calf muscle is located at the back of your lower leg.

1 Stand up straight and put one foot about 12 inches (30 centimeters) ahead of the other.

2 Raise the toes of your forward foot as far as you can, keeping your heel firmly on the floor. Hold this position for a count of ten.

3 Repeat the stretch using your other leg.

SHOULDER ROLLS

1 Stand up straight with your hands by your sides.

2 Roll your shoulders in a backward direction, making as big a circle as you can. Do ten rolls.

3 Repeat the exercise, rolling your shoulders forward this time.

BREAKFALLS

Many people who are new to judo are afraid of falling or being thrown. This makes them stiffen up, which makes it more likely that the fall will hurt. So the first thing to learn in judo is how to break, or soften, a fall. You do this by rolling, tumbling, and using your arms to absorb the shock. These breakfall techniques, also called *ukemi,* take the force out of the impact. Practicing breakfalls builds up your confidence and lessens your fear of being thrown.

PRACTICING BREAKFALLS

It is best to practice breakfalls on your own at first. Two easy techniques are shown here. Always use a judo mat to practice breakfalls. Most beginners find it easier to fall either to their right or left side. In competitions, you will be thrown to either side, so it is really important to practice your breakfalls on both sides.

As your confidence grows, you can practice breakfalls with a partner. At first it is very important that the thrower guide his or her partner onto the mat, trying to help the partner learn.

JUDO MATS

As soon as you start falling, you will realize how important the judo mat, or *tatami,* is. *Tatamis* are no longer made of traditional Japanese rice-straw matting, but they are specially made to take some of the force out of falls. At first, a special crash-mat may also be used. Always practice on the judo mat, and always practice with a qualified instructor nearby.

BACK BREAKFALL

1 Stand with your arms straight out in front of you.

2 Bend your knees and go into a squatting position as you let yourself fall backward. Tuck your chin in and curve your back as you start to fall.

3 Slap down hard with the palms of both hands, keeping your head up and off the mat. The harder you slap, the easier the landing.

SIDE BREAKFALL

1 Squat down on the mat and look straight ahead. Put your right arm out and thrust your right leg forward and diagonally across your body.

2 Roll to the right. As your bottom touches the mat, strike the mat with your right arm. Keep your chin tucked in and your head off the mat.

THROWING

Throwing techniques form the basis of judo. Most of the throws rely more on skill and timing than on strength. The *judoka* performing the throw usually tries to move his or her partner into an unbalanced position. This makes the throw much easier. Groups of throws are named according to which part of the body the thrower uses to gain power. In judo, there are hip techniques, hand techniques, and foot-and-leg techniques. Beginners go through the moves slowly, learning them step by step, and then putting all the steps together in one smooth action.

NAMES OF THROWS AND THROWERS

Groups of throws and individual techniques all have a Japanese and an English name. These may seem difficult at first, but you will soon pick them up. Hip techniques are called *koshi-waza* and hand techniques are called *te-waza*.

In judo, Japanese terms are used for the two partners, or opponents. The *judoka* performing a move such as a throw is called the *tori*. The partner who is on the receiving end of the move is called the *uke*.

MAJOR HIP THROW

This throw, called *o-goshi* in Japanese, is one of the most commonly used first throws for beginners. It is one of the hip techniques. The thrower uses a powerful hip action to lift his or her opponent up and over.

1 Step across in front of the *uke* with your right foot as you grip his or her sleeve with your left hand.

2 Move your right hand around the *uke's* back, bend your knees, and pull the *uke's* hip against your back.

3 Straighten your legs, bend forward, and pull the *uke* over your hips and back. Keep hold of the *uke's* sleeve with your right hand to help soften his or her fall.

BODY DROP

The body drop, or *tai-otoshi,* is one of the hand techniques. The *tori* uses his or her hands to get the *uke* moving and unbalance him or her. Hand techniques are especially useful for small *judokas* and have a high scoring rate in competition.

First push the *uke* backward. When the *uke* pushes back, pull him or her forward. Then turn to the left, placing your right calf across the *uke's* right ankle, and throw him or her across your leg.

FOOT-AND-LEG THROWS

Most foot-and-leg techniques involve throwing the opponent by moving one leg out from under him or her. This may be done using a sweeping, hooking, or tripping action, especially when the opponent is least expecting it or is off balance. Timing is very important. Foot-and-leg throws should only be practiced with an instructor, since he or she will help you get the timing right.

FOULS

You are never allowed to kick in judo, so you must learn to perform the foot-and-leg techniques correctly. The techniques are all part of the overall group of throws and involve sweeping the opponent, not kicking or tripping at random. Attempting to throw an opponent by wrapping a leg around his or her leg is also a foul in judo.

FOOT SWEEP

In the advancing foot sweep, or *deashi-barai,* you force your opponent to take a step forward and then sweep the *uke's* foot away.

1 Push forward against your partner. Then step backward to make him or her follow you.

2 As the *uke* steps forward onto his or her left foot, sweep it away with the sole of your right foot, just as the *uke* is about to put his or her weight on it. At the same time, pull down and out on his or her sleeve with your right hand.

3 If your timing is right, the *uke* will go down as if he or she has slipped on a banana peel. Remember to make a big, bold, sweeping action from the hip, not just a little tap with the foot.

FOOT REAP

In the major inner reap, or *o-uchi-gari*, the attacker drives forward off the back foot and uses the other leg to reap, which means to cut or clip, one of the *uke's* legs to throw him or her backward.

The major inner reap, shown here, is a kind of foot reap.

LEG THROW

The inner thigh throw, or *uchi-mata,* is one of the most successful and popular moves in judo. However, it is only used by senior *judokas* and requires a lot of practice to get the timing exactly right. The *tori* turns toward the *uke,* steps between his or her legs, and sweeps upward with the

forward leg against the *uke's* inside thigh. The *uke* is thrown over the forward leg and lands on his or her back.

The inner thigh throw is a kind of leg throw.

GROUNDWORK

In competitive judo for beginners, a player can win by bringing his or her opponent to the ground with a throw or by holding the opponent down on the mat. Moves made on the mat are called groundwork, and usually involve **grappling** for position and holding the opponent down.

For beginners and juniors, groundwork is made up of **hold-downs.** These involve pinning the opponent down and holding that position for up to 25 seconds. The opponent will try to wriggle free, and you might think that he or she will be able to do so if the person is heavier or stronger than you are. But in judo, skillful techniques can be used to overcome sheer strength, especially when you are using body positions correctly.

SCARF HOLD

This head-and-shoulder pin is one of the first hold-downs to learn. It is called *kesa-gatame* in Japanese and is named after the traditional scarf, or diagonal sash, that was worn in ancient Japan. In fact, Japanese archers still wear the *kesa*. The name comes from the diagonal hold you put on your opponent.

1 Your opponent has fallen at your side. Quickly drop down and sit in the space between his or her right arm and body, holding his or her shoulders with both of your hands. Wedge your hip tightly against the *uke's* body as you put your right arm around his or her neck.

2 Grip your opponent's jacket tightly with both hands, and spread your legs wide to keep yourself stable. Lower your head, and hold your opponent in that position.

LEARNING ABOUT ARMLOCKS AND STRANGLEHOLDS

There are two more techniques that only seniors should use. These are armlocks and strangleholds. They can be dangerous, so there are many rules about how to use them properly. Juniors are not allowed to use them, so do not try any of the armlocks or strangleholds that you see seniors using.

Kate Howey of Great Britain, in the blue gi, used an armlock to win a match at the 2000 Olympic Games in Sydney.

KNOWING WHEN TO STOP

To stop groundwork, the defender taps on the mat or the attacker's body twice. When this happens, or if the defender shows in any other way that they want you to stop, you must release the defender immediately.

SACRIFICE THROWS AND COMBINATIONS

After learning basic throws and groundwork, *judokas* learn more advanced throws and ways to combine moves. In a sacrifice throw, the *judoka* appears to sacrifice, or give up, a good position. In fact, the *judoka* uses the throw to gain a different, unexpected advantage. Sacrifice throws usually involve going down on the mat onto one's back or side and throwing the opponent with one's legs. They can be exciting to watch, and they are a good move for beginners to practice. Remember, though, that sacrifices can leave you open to attack if they are not done well in a competition.

SACRIFICE THROW

Tomoe-nage, sometimes called a stomach throw, often earns high scores in competitions. It is useful when your opponent has tried a move such as a foot reap but has failed.

1 Drop down onto your back as you hold onto your opponent's jacket. Pull the *uke* toward you, raise your leg, and then center your foot on his or her stomach.

2 Straighten your leg sharply and hang onto the *uke's* jacket so that he or she whirls over you onto his or her back.

Timing is very important in this move so that you do not hurt yourself or your opponent. You must remember also that it is a risky move, because if you fail to throw your opponent, he or she could easily drop down and put you in a **hold-down** such as the scarf hold.

COMBINATION THROWING TECHNIQUES

You can also practice putting two or more throws together. This will be useful when you are ready to compete. Double moves are called linked techniques, *renzoku-waza*, when they are done in the same direction. They are called combination techniques, *renraku-waza*, when the first technique, which breaks the opponent's balance, is done in one direction, and the second is done in the other direction.

Some of the throws already described can be used in combinations. A good example would be to try the body drop shown on page 17, and if it does not work, switch into a major inner reap in the other direction, as on page 19.

These students are combining the body drop and a major inner reap. Step 1 is the attempted body drop.

When that fails, the judoka switches to Step 2—the major inner reap.

DEFENSE BECOMES ATTACK

In all competitive sports, players must learn to defend as well as attack. In judo, however, defense is always seen as an opportunity to **counter-attack.** Competition rules state that it is an offense, or cause for penalty, to take up too defensive an attitude, either by backing away or by not attacking. This rule and the whole attitude of attack make judo fun to learn, practice, and watch.

COUNTER-ATTACK

For every judo move there is a counter-move. Some moves are more difficult to counter than others. You will learn this with experience. You will also learn that it is much easier to counter a move by your opponent if it is badly timed or incorrectly performed. Likewise, you have to time your counter-attack well for it to be successful.

You can counter-attack just as your opponent shifts his or her balance to attack you. Or you can wait until the attack is under way. For example, you could block an inner thigh throw like the one on page 19, and counter with a body drop like the one on page 17. You can also reverse the order of these moves.

Here is a very simple, but effective counter-attack.

1 Your opponent tries a foot sweep. You see it coming and quickly lift your foot.

2 The opponent's foot passes under yours.

3 Help your opponent's foot on its way in the same direction. This will throw him or her off-balance.

FREE PRACTICE

The best way to improve your skills in defending and counter-attacking is during free practice, or *randori*, when you compete against an opponent. It is called "free" because it is not pre-planned and does not involve **drills.** *Randori* gives players an opportunity to practice their skills in a competitive situation. There is no referee, so it is up to the two partners to help each other practice and learn.

Sometimes judo clubs also organize a session of practice competitions with rules and points strictly enforced. This gives more advanced *judokas* the experience of serious competition.

Most dojos offer free practice sessions.

! COOLING DOWN

It is important to cool down gently after any vigorous exercise. You can do this by jogging or walking, and gently stretching. Cool-down exercises are similar to the warm-up exercises on pages 12 and 13. Some *judokas* like to extend their cool down by doing some *kata* exercises to music.

GRADING

When you join a judo club, you should become a member of the National Judo Association. As a member of the National Judo Association you will receive information about judo activities and training camps in your state. You will also get updates on what is happening in the International Judo Federation.

Your membership also gives you the right to be graded and promoted properly, and to attend regional and national competitions when you are ready. As you work your way from beginner to expert, your level of skill is shown by different colored belts. When you are wearing your belt, everyone can see which level you have reached.

BELT RANKS

Grades and belt colors vary in different countries—one system is shown in the box below. Each grade, called a *mon*, has its own distinctive belt. In the United States, belt colors for the junior grades usually progress in the following order: white, yellow, orange, green, blue, and purple.

	Junior Grades		
Mon	*Belt color*	*Mon*	*Belt color*
1st	white, one red bar	10th	green, one red bar
2nd	white, two red bars	11th	green, two red bars
3rd	white, three red bars	12th	green, three red bars
4th	yellow, one red bar	13th	blue, one red bar
5th	yellow, two red bars	14th	blue, two red bars
6th	yellow, three red bars	15th	blue, three red bars
7th	orange, one red bar	16th	brown, one red bar
8th	orange, two red bars	17th	brown, two red bars
9th	orange, three red bars	18th	brown, three red bars

Seniors are usually aged seventeen and over. One system, with a series of nine grades, called *kyu*, is shown below.

Senior Grades			
Kyu	*Belt color*	*Kyu*	*Belt color*
9th	yellow	4th	blue
8th	orange	3rd	blue
7th	orange	2nd	brown
6th	green	1st	brown
5th	green		black

In the United States, most senior *judokas* progress in the following order: white, yellow, green, brown, black. The brown belt is broken down into three different grades, or *kyu*. The black belt is split up into ten different grades, or *dan*.

GRADING EXAMS

To move up a grade and gain a new belt, you have to take a grading exam. This is usually in two parts, covering practice and theory. There is a competition section as well as a set of questions about judo to answer.

You must pass a grading exam to advance.

Grades are important in judo. Juniors must always show respect for seniors. However, expert *judokas* show total respect for lower grades and beginners too. This is an important aspect of all the martial arts. Do not worry about which belt color you wear. Do the best you can, and you will move up at your own pace.

A WORLD SPORT

Judo became a serious competitive sport in 1930 when the first All-Japan Championships were held in Tokyo. After judo grew in popularity around the world, the International Judo Federation was founded in 1951. The first World Championships were held five years later.

Judo first became an Olympic sport for male competitors in 1964, at the Tokyo Games. The first Olympic gold medal in judo was won by Japan, when Takehide Nakatani won the lightweight class. However, his 15,000 Japanese supporters at home were shocked when a Dutchman, Anton Geesink, beat the Japanese favorite for the open category. Women's judo was added as an Olympic sport at the 1992 Barcelona Games.

CONTEST RULES

Judo sporting contests take place on a 8¾-yard- (8-meter-) square mat with a safety area around it. Each match is controlled by a referee in the contest area, and two judges, who remain at opposite corners outside the danger area. A men's match lasts five minutes, a women's match lasts four minutes, and junior matches last three minutes. A timekeeper times the match and the length of each hold.

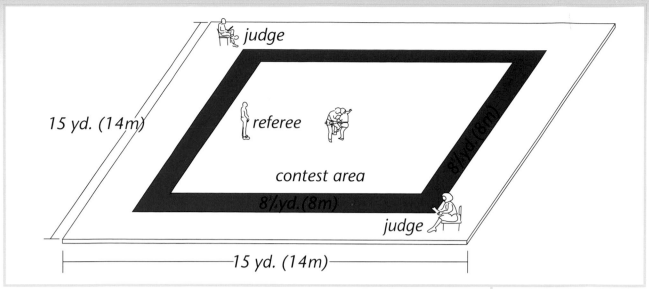

judge

15 yd. (14m)

referee

contest area

8¼ yd. (8m)

8¼ yd. (8m)

judge

15 yd. (14m)

One contestant wears a red or blue sash, and the other wears a white one. This helps the officials and spectators tell them apart. It is now becoming regular practice for one of them to wear a blue *judogi* and the other to wear a white one. To win the match, a player has to score an *ippon,* or two *waza-aris.* If neither achieves this, points are added up according to the number of *waza-aris, yukos,* and *kokas* scored. This is explained in the table below. One *waza-ari* beats any number of *yukos,* and one *yuko* beats any number of *kokas.* If the match is a tie, the referee and judges decide on the winner.

This diagram shows the contest area for an international competition.

Score	Technique
ippon	skillful throw resulting in opponent landing with speed and force on back; opponent **submits** to armlock or stranglehold; 25-second **hold-down**
waza-ari	throw that lacks speed or force, or in which the opponent lands partially on the back; 20- to 24-second hold-down
yuko	throw that lacks speed or force, or the opponent lands on side; 15- to 19-second hold-down
koka	throw from which opponent lands on thigh or buttocks; 10- to 14-second hold-down

Penalty points are deducted from the players' scores if they break any rules.

JAPANESE WORDS

The Japanese words are pronounced as written here. When you see the letters *ai*, say them like the English word *eye*.

Japanese word	Meaning	Japanese word	Meaning
deashi-barai	advancing foot reap	*renzoku-waza*	linked technique
dojo	training hall	*samurai*	Japanese warrior
ippon	one full point	*sensei*	judo instructor, teacher
judoji	judo uniform		
judoka	student of judo	*tai-otoshi*	body drop
jujitsu	a martial art, means "gentle skill"	*tatami*	mat
		te-waza	hand technique
kata	pattern, form	*tomoe-nage*	stomach throw
kesa-gatame	scarf hold	*tori*	in a pair of judo students, the one performing a move
Kodokan	judo school, means "the place for studying the way"	*uchi-mata*	inner thigh throw
koka	lowest judo score, means "valuable"	*uke*	in a pair of judo students, the one on the receiving end of a move
koshi-waza	hip technique		
kyu	grade		
mon	junior grade	*ukemi*	breakfall techniques
o-goshi	major hip throw	*waza-ari*	a half point
o-uchi-gari	major inner reap	*yuko*	the third highest judo score, means "valid"
randori	free practice		
renraku-waza	combination technique		

GLOSSARY

counter-attack — to respond to an attack by an opponent with your own attack

drill — repeating something to help you learn it

grappling — gripping and wrestling with an opponent

hold-down — move in which a judo student holds his or her opponent down on the ground

imperial — having to do with an empire. The imperial capital was the capital of the Japanese Empire.

philosophy — set of beliefs, often designed to help people be good or become wise

submit — to give up, especially when you are held down and cannot move (The noun form of *submit* is *submission*.)

MORE BOOKS TO READ

Brousse, Michael and David Matsumoto. *Judo: A Sport and a Way of Life.* Seoul, Korea: International Judo Federation, 1999.

Matsumoto, David. *An Introduction to Kodokan Judo: History and Philosophy.* Tokyo, Japan: Hon-No-Toshoma, 1996.

Nardi, Thomas J. *Karate and Judo.* Austin, Tex.: Raintree Steck-Vaughn Publishers, 1996.

Randall, Pamela. *Judo.* New York: Rosen Publishing Group, Inc., 1999.

TAKING IT FURTHER

International Judo Federation
21st Floor Doosan Building 101–1 Ulchiro 1ka Choong Ku
Seoul, South Korea

Kodokan Judo Institute
1-16-30 Kasuga, Bunkyo-ku
Tokyo 112-0003 Japan

United States Judo, Inc.
1 Olympic Plaza, Suite 202
Colorado Springs, CO 80909
Telephone: (719) 578-4730

INDEX

ink noted
2.3.08 YP